WHEN THE SPIRIT Comes

AN OVERVIEW OF ACTS

JACK HAYFORD
SCOTT BAUER • JACK HAMILTON

WHEN THE SPIRIT COMES
A Practical, Introductory Guidebook for a Comprehensive Overview in the Bible Book of ACTS

Copyright © 1996, 2001 Living Way Ministries.

All rights reserved. No part of this publication may be reproduced, stored in a retrieval system, or transmitted in any form by any means without the prior permission of the publisher.

Unless otherwise noted, all Scripture references are from the New King James Version:
Copyright © 1979, 1980, 1982 by Thomas Nelson, Inc., Nashville, Tennessee.
Maps and illustrations taken from the *Nelson's Complete Book of Bible Maps and Charts*, ©1993, Thomas Nelson, Inc. Used by permission.
Outline of Acts taken from the *Spirit-Filled Life Bible*, ©1991, Thomas Nelson, Inc. Used by permission.

Photographs of Dr. Jack Hayford and Dr. Scott Bauer by Danick Studios
Photograph of Dr. Jack Hamilton by Brian Aveni Photography.

Published by Living Way Ministries
14300 Sherman Way
Van Nuys, CA (USA) 91405-2499
(818) 779-8400 • (800) 776-8180

ISBN 0-916847-19-5
Printed in Colombia
by Editorial Buena Semilla.

TABLE OF CONTENTS

Growing With the Bible Book-A-Month   4

Introducing the Bible Book of Acts   9

An Outline of Acts   11

Part 1:
The Pillar Principles of Acts   13

Part 2:
The Relevant Answers in Acts   29

Part 3:
Practical Wisdom from Acts   49

Ministry Resources   66

FRONTPIECE

GROWING WITH THE BIBLE BOOK-A-MONTH STUDIES

Disciples of the Lord Jesus Christ know it: *There is no substitute for the Word of God in our daily lives!* Still, many find that the formation of a satisfying, fulfilling discipline in reading and studying God's Word is not easy. In contrast, many fall into a merely regimented or legalistic habit that eventually withers for lack of the Holy Spirit's breath upon it. Others have difficulty finding direction or maintaining focus; besides, we all need help to keep us moving forward *through* the Word.

The formulation of the "Bible Book-A-Month" concept was born in the heart of Dr. Jack Hayford, who, as a pastor, constantly seeks improved means of helping people achieve three things: *systematic*, *substantial,* and *thorough* coverage of the Bible. Each is important to accomplish the objective of good Bible study, and they can be realized through this plan.

(1) It's <u>systematic</u>, by reason of the *month-by-month* advancement of the program; (2) it's <u>substantial</u>, because of the *spiritual weight* of the triangular

approach of study employed; and (3) it's <u>thorough</u>, for *every book* of the Bible is incorporated in it.

THE TRIANGULAR APPROACH

There are many worthwhile approaches to a study of the Holy Bible. For example, "synthetic" study—which draws together highlights to provide a quick grasp of a book; "critical" study—which assesses the ancient textual resources that authenticate the trustworthiness of the book as a document; or "verse-by-verse" study—which seeks to exhaust every book of the totality of its content.

Distinct from any of these, the "Bible Book-A-Month" study seeks to achieve the maximum possible grasp of a book's truth while keeping a pace forward which sustains the average Bible student's interest. It is <u>demanding</u> enough in its *academics* to seriously engage those interested in intelligent, thought-provoking study. Yet it is <u>dynamic</u> enough in its *movement* to avoid losing passion, and to keep each student at a point of continuous anticipation. This is done through use of a **"triangular approach"** to each book—which focuses the three primary things to be found in every book of the Bible.

1. Each Bible book contains an *essential message*: the core concepts which distinguish that book and provide its place in God's Word. This is found in *towering truths* and *pillar passages* within that book. These together provide a rich overview of the Holy Spirit's theme and thrust in that book of the Bible.

2. Each Bible book presents *problems* and evokes *questions* rising from the need to integrate that book's content with the whole Bible, as well as to interpret its content as it addresses current issues. Good Bible study helps questioners find *satisfactory answers* to reasoned inquiry, even as it demonstrates the *relevancy* of God's Word to today's social problems. Thus, we discover the power of the Holy Spirit—present to reveal Christ to the world—TODAY!

3. Each Bible book provides *practical wisdom* and *personal guidance*; it sheds light on the believer's daily walk and service as he or she follows Jesus Christ. Healthy study in God's Word should provide *information* and *inspiration*, but only as it issues in *incarnation* does it achieve its goal! In each book, *insights for faithful, fruitful pathways* will show how to adopt, adapt, and apply the Bible to your life, as Jesus' disciple.

These perspectives provide the viewpoints which "triangulate" on the text: each book studied through three lessons which unfold the truth of God's Word noting one of the above three values. The "Bible Book-A-Month" triangular approach works this way:

- Dr. Jack Hayford's presentation is first, providing a full picture of the purpose and message of each book.

- Dr. Scott Bauer's lesson is second, affording a grasp of the relevancy of each book and revealing the Spirit's power as it unveils Jesus Himself.

- Dr. Jack Hamilton's lesson is third in each volume, presenting the practical lessons of each book.

By means of these three lessons, a comprehensive overview of a book (or books) of the Bible is presented in each study, so it can be truly gained, grasped, and applied.

TRIPLE TOOLS—SUPPORT RESOURCES

1. Each Bible book, and the studies as originally presented, will be available on audio cassettes. Because Pastor Hayford has been asked by a national distributor of audio Bibles to record the whole of the Scriptures in the New King James Version, the text being studied is on tape. These audio Bibles are being produced now, and each correlated reading will be released in conjunction with the "Bible Book-A-Month" program (Fall 1996 through Spring 1998).
2. Audio cassettes of the three lessons are also available with each study guide. These contain the complete teachings by Drs. Hayford, Bauer, and Hamilton and will become available as they are produced from month to month.
3. The above two join with the entire set of books (like this one) to complete the support resources for the "Bible Book-A-Month" studies. Additional resources, noted in each volume, may also be ordered by calling Living Way Ministries at 800-776-8180.

ACTS:
THE KEY WORDS ARE "EMPOWERED FOR WITNESS"

This book could be regarded as "The Acts of the Spirit of Christ working in and through the Apostles." Luke's strong emphasis in the book of Acts is on the ministry of the Holy Spirit.

KEY VERSES

"But you shall receive power when the Holy Spirit has come upon you; and you shall be witnesses to Me in Jerusalem, and in all Judea and Samaria, and to the end of the earth." Acts 1:8

"And they continued steadfastly in the apostles' doctrine and fellowship, in the breaking of bread, and in prayers. ...praising God and having favor with all the people. And the Lord added to the church daily those who were being saved." Acts 2:42-47

KEY CHAPTER: ACTS 2

Chapter 2 records the earth-changing events of the Day of Pentecost when the Holy Spirit comes, fulfilling Christ's command to wait until the Holy Spirit arrives to empower and direct the witness. The Spirit transforms a small group of fearful men and women into a thriving, worldwide church that is ever moving forward and fulfilling the Great Commission.

Introducing the Bible Book of
ACTS

Author: Historically, Luke
Date: About A.D. 62
Theme: The Work of the Holy Spirit in the Early History of Christianity
Key Words: Jesus, Spirit, Resurrection, Apostle, Church

AUTHOR

The Book of Acts does not specifically mention its author, but many indicators point to Luke, "the beloved physician" (Colossians 4:14). The writer was a man of culture, as indicated by his literary style; he had a universal outlook; and he revealed an interest in medical matters. In addition, church tradition uniformly declares that Luke was the author of Acts.

DATE

Luke tells the story of the early church within the framework of first century geographical, political, and historical details. There is no mention of the fall of Jerusalem or Nero's persecution of the Christians. Because the book does not record the death of Paul but leaves him a prisoner in Rome, it is logical to date the writing of Acts near the end of the apostle's imprisonment there in about 62 A.D.

The Nations of
PENTECOST

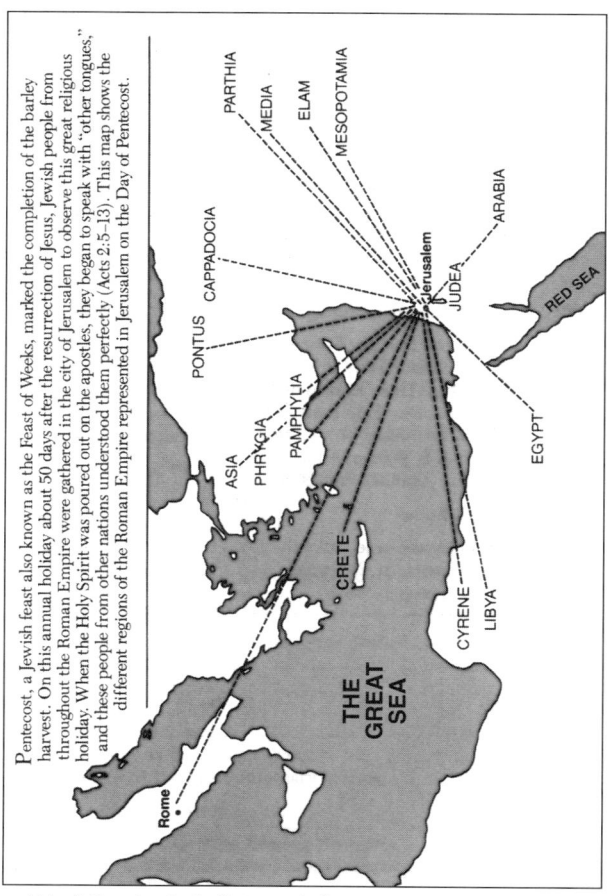

Pentecost, a Jewish feast also known as the Feast of Weeks, marked the completion of the barley harvest. On this annual holiday about 50 days after the resurrection of Jesus, Jewish people from throughout the Roman Empire were gathered in the city of Jerusalem to observe this great religious holiday. When the Holy Spirit was poured out on the apostles, they began to speak with "other tongues," and these people from other nations understood them perfectly (Acts 2:5–13). This map shows the different regions of the Roman Empire represented in Jerusalem on the Day of Pentecost.

Nelson's Complete Book of Maps and Charts © 1993, Thomas Nelson, Inc.

AN OUTLINE OF ACTS

Prologue   1:1-14

Part One: Peter and the ministry of the Jewish church in Jerusalem   1:15-12:24

I.	The selection of Matthias as the twelfth apostle	1:15-26
II.	The pentecostal outpouring of the Holy Spirit	2:1-47
III.	The healing of the lame man	3:1-4:31
IV.	Apostolic authority in the early church	4:32-5:42
V.	The ministry of Stephen	6:1-7:60
VI.	The first ministry to non-Jews	8:1-40
VII.	The conversion of Saul	9:1-31
VIII.	Aeneas and Dorcas healed through Peter's ministry	9:32-43
IX.	The story of Cornelius	10:1-11:18
X.	The witness of the early church	11:19-12:24

Part Two: Paul and the international outreach of the church at Antioch   12:25-28:31

I.	Paul's first missionary journey	12:25-14:28
II.	The Council at Jerusalem to discuss law and grace	15:1-35
III.	Paul's second missionary journey	15:36-18:22
IV.	Paul's third missionary journey	18:23-21:14
V.	Paul's journey to Rome through Jerusalem	21:15-28:31

When the Events in
ACTS OCCURRED

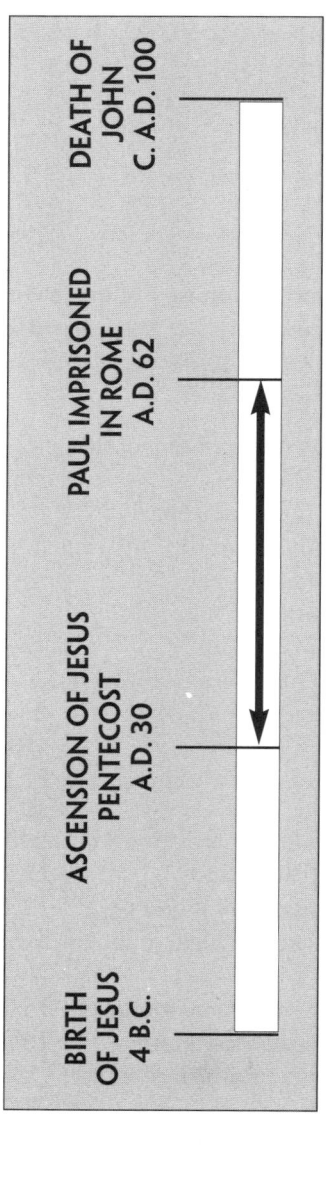

| BIRTH OF JESUS 4 B.C. | ASCENSION OF JESUS PENTECOST A.D. 30 | PAUL IMPRISONED IN ROME A.D. 62 | DEATH OF JOHN C. A.D. 100 |

Acts shows Jesus as still at work through His Church by the power of the Holy Spirit.

PART 1

THE PILLAR PRINCIPLES OF ACTS

JACK HAYFORD

Peter's
TRAVELS

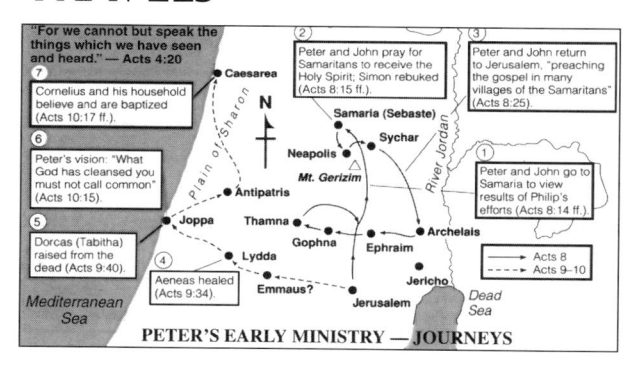

"For we cannot but speak the things which we have seen and heard." — Acts 4:20

7 Cornelius and his household believe and are baptized (Acts 10:17 ff.)

6 Peter's vision: "What God has cleansed you must not call common" (Acts 10:15).

5 Dorcas (Tabitha) raised from the dead (Acts 9:40).

4 Aeneas healed (Acts 9:34).

2 Peter and John pray for Samaritans to receive the Holy Spirit; Simon rebuked (Acts 8:15 ff.)

3 Peter and John return to Jerusalem, "preaching the gospel in many villages of the Samaritans" (Acts 8:25).

1 Peter and John go to Samaria to view results of Philip's efforts (Acts 8:14 ff.).

— Acts 8
--- Acts 9–10

PETER'S EARLY MINISTRY — JOURNEYS

Philip's
TRAVELS

5 Philip lives in Caesarea with his four virgin daughters, who are prophetesses. They are visited there by Paul (Acts 21:8 ff.).

"And the multitudes with one accord heeded the things spoken by Philip, hearing and seeing the miracles which he did." —Acts 8:6

2 Philip travels to "the city of Samaria," where Simon the sorcerer is converted (Acts 8:4 ff.).

4 "Found at Azotus," Philip preaches from city to city until he reaches Caesarea (Acts 8:40).

1 Philip becomes a deacon with six others (Acts 6:5).

3 The road from Jerusalem to Gaza: Philip baptizes the Ethiopian eunuch (Acts 8:26 ff.).

PHILIP'S TRAVELS

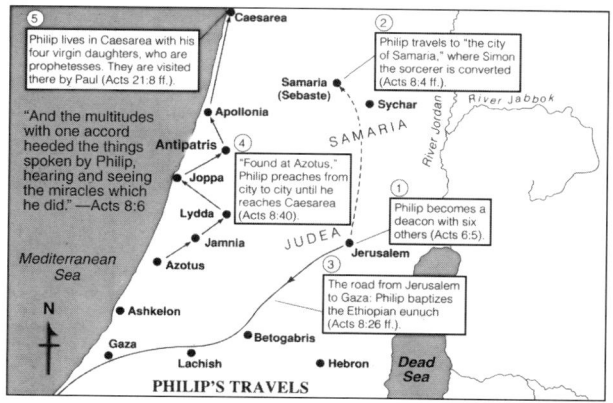

Nelson's Complete Book of Maps and Charts © 1993, Thomas Nelson, Inc.

The Pillar Principles of
ACTS

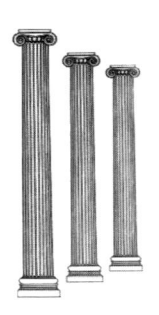

No words could more aptly describe the Book of Acts than the title of this study guide, *"**When the Spirit Comes.**"* The breath of heaven sweeps in and around the pages of the eternal record of the young church Jesus birthed at Pentecost by pouring out the Holy Spirit from heaven.

From the holy sound of "a rushing mighty wind" on that day (chapter 2), to the hellish cries of demons coming out of people in Samaria (chapter 8), to the stormy winds of the tempest which drove Paul on a ship across half the Mediterranean Sea, the ***breath*** of God's Spirit is the source of action. He fills the humble soul, drives back the powers of hell and executes the will of God—all to the glory of Jesus!

"And you shall receive power," were more than casually spoken words. The resurrected Lord was issuing a promise that would insure that all He "began to do and teach" (1:1) would be continued—<u>through</u> His people and <u>by</u> His power.

The Book of Acts reports the phenomenon of Jesus Christ: God incarnate in a human body, now Lord and Savior of the Church, becoming God incarnate in a "body" called His Church. In the opening words of his historical treatise, Luke—the writer of Acts—is saying, *"What Jesus both began to do and teach, He is now continuing to do in and teach through His own people—the living organism of the Holy Spirit-filled Church."*

To study Acts is to gain a glimpse of God's idea for reaching the whole world with His love and grace. Jesus sets the target, aiming for *"Jerusalem, Judea, Samaria and to the end of the earth"* (1:8). Then He sets His hand, pouring forth the promise of the Holy Spirit, which Peter described to onlookers as that "promise…which you now see and hear" (2:33).

So, we are introduced to the Holy Spirit as God—the Third Person of the Trinity—fully present to empower the redeemed and to enable them to minister exactly what Jesus would minister, for the same anointing was present.

Open Acts and read it through in its entirety—spend about two hours and experience what J. B. Phillips described. When asked how he felt as he labored over his contemporary translation of Acts, he said, *"I felt like I was trying to rewire an entire house with the power left on all the time!"* A quick but earnest reading of this book immediately discloses two things about the author's intent:

- Luke focuses full attention on the Holy Spirit's working, making direct reference to Him 53 times—"the Holy Spirit" (42 times) or "the Spirit" (11 times). The record may be titled the "Acts of the Apostles," but the action is the result of one Source above all: The Spirit of the Living God, glorifying Jesus as the Messiah, the Son of God.

- Luke outlines his summary of the early Church's life and action using Jesus' words in chapter 1:8 prophesying the promised spread of the Gospel geographically and ethnically—(a) "to Jerusalem" (chapters 2-7), (b) "to Judea and Samaria" (chapters 8-12), and (c) "to the uttermost parts of the earth" (chapters 13-28).

Let us open our hearts to this magnificent disclosure of holy history, with a readiness to allow a reproduction of its glory in our lives. Take Acts in hand with a readiness to inhale!! Breathe deeply of its fullest possibilities for personal transformation and power, flowing from a heart of ready obedience and receptivity.

> *"For the promise is to you and to your children, and to all who are afar off, as many as the Lord our God will call."*
> Acts 2:39

Acts' CENTRAL PERSONALITIES

Besides the Person of the Holy Spirit and His tireless and relentless focus on the Person of Jesus, there are two key personalities around whom Luke fashions the Acts of the Apostles.

PETER

He is the primary spokesperson for the twelve, who rises to speak at Pentecost (2:14); who preaches the first sermons in this book (2:14-40; 3:12-26; 4:8-11); and around whom most early miracles are seen (3:4; 5:3, 9, 15; 8:14, 15; 9:32-42; 10:1-48; 12:1-18).

PAUL

He is the chosen instrument of the Lord for the spread of the Gospel to the Gentiles. After his conversion (chapter 9:3-22), which is preceded by his intense persecution of the early church (chapters 7:58; 8:1-3; 9:1-2), Paul is central to the remainder of Acts (chapters 13-28).

(In your reading, take notes and reference the role of added pivotal personalities in Acts.)

1. John
2. James (2)
3. Philip
4. Stephen
5. Barnabas
6. Silas
7. Ananias
8. Cornelius
9. Agabus
10. Timothy
11. Herod (2)
12. Felix, Festus

TWELVE KEY CONCEPTS

The content of Acts distills around a dozen key concepts which we, in our studies, refer to as the ***pillar principles*** of each book. They are the foundational ideas which provide the grid of truth which is conveyed to us for our understanding and practice. For clarity and simplicity, we have divided these under three ideas:

- **The ENERGY at Work IN ACTS**
  These four points summarize the primary "forces" that are shaping the movement of God through the vital life of the Church.

- **The ELEMENTS of Witness IN ACTS**
  These four points indicate primary "attributes" of the vital life of the Church which contribute to its health, its style and its spread.

- **The ENVIRONMENT of Harvest IN ACTS**
  These four points focus the primary "tensions" which constrain the Church, shaping its life and sharpening its vital, cutting edge.

THE ENERGY AT WORK IN ACTS

1. The Overflowing Promise of the Fullness of God's Holy Spirit

From the beginning, Jesus' promise in 1:8 is intended to be realized by all the followers of the Lord (2:38). What happens on the Day of Pentecost, at the inception of the Church, is affirmed to ever be the verifiable portion of all.

When Peter reports what happened at the house of Cornelius, when the first Gentiles to receive the Holy Spirit spoke "with tongues and prophesied" (10:48), he gives this description: "the Holy Spirit fell upon them as upon us at the beginning" (11:15). This becomes the manifest evidence to the bewildered Jerusalem believers who, until then, were uncertain of the reality experienced by the Gentiles.

The earlier insistence of the apostles that ministry be extended to the new believers in Samaria indicates a steadfast priority. Each convert needs to "receive the Holy Spirit" as well as receive the message of salvation in Christ Jesus (8:14-15). Paul exhibits a similar concern at Ephesus, where Apollos' solid, biblical teaching had garnered converts, but who still knew little or nothing about the Holy Spirit's ministry to and through each believer (19:1-6).

Besides "receiving" the Holy Spirit, the text of Acts reveals that continuous "refilling" is appropriate and necessary. Examine these cases and ask the Lord to pour something fresh of His Spirit into the vessel of your own life: 4:8; 4:31; 13:39. (In this regard, note Ephesians 5:17-20.)

2. The Overwhelming Demonstration of God's Displayed Power

With the advent of the Holy Spirit, "signs and wonders" are not only present, but are announced as normative to the whole era of the Spirit's work in the Church (2:19). As with the "tongues" at Pentecost, which brought a mixed response of mocking on one hand and interest and inquiry on the other (2:1-13), so the habits of humanity continue in every age. There are three striking facts about signs and wonders in the early Church:

a. They are present at times of spiritual breakthrough and evangelistic thrust, and are never seen as an end in themselves (2:43; 5:12; 8:13; 14:13).

b. They are prayed for, not as a sensation-seeking quest, but as a Christ-glorifying goal (4:30).

c. They are of an unpredictable variety; suited to the need of the situation and not necessarily to be replicated elsewhere, yet still fulfilling the unlimiting word of Jesus' prophecy about "greater works" (e.g. 8:39; 13:11; 19:12—see John 14:12).

3. The Overcoming Preaching of God's Eternal Word in the Scriptures

One scholar has noted Acts 19:6 as the watershed text of the entire book: "So the word of the Lord grew mightily and prevailed." This is not a necessary conclusion in rightly assessing the flow of the Acts narrative, but it is certainly a telling observation. *Everywhere* throughout the book, "the Word" is the key to the release of power. Jesus promised the Holy Spirit as the source of power, but His working comes only as confirmation when "the Word" is proclaimed (see Mark 16:19-20).

Using a concordance, look up all references to "the word" or "the Scriptures" in Acts, also noting the frequency with which Old Testament passages are quoted (e.g. 1:20; 2:17-21; 2:25-28; 2:34-35; 3:22, 25; 4:25-26; Stephen's whole sermon in chapter 7; 8:31-32; etc.). Study how the text of Scripture is used to establish authority as well as to provide insight. What lessons do you draw from this habit?

4. The Overarching Sense of God's Sovereign Grace Intervening

There is a manifest humility in the whole of the record of Acts, which indicates that the disciples knew they were not the "achievers" of what occurred, but that they were the "believers" who opened to what *God* was <u>doing</u>! Examine such references as 2:23; 2:47; 3:18; 10:45-47; 11:17-18; 12:5-11; 15:18, etc.

It is refreshing to see the blend of a sound theology that focuses on God's greatness, yet still maintains the importance of human participation with His plan. This balance is a key to the dynamic life of believers in the early Church: they knew their source of life and power was not self-generated or promoted; but they grew as they earnestly pursued God's power in their lives through prayer and ministered that power by pursuing paths of outreach and service.

THE ELEMENTS OF WITNESS IN
ACTS

5. The Testimony of Jesus

The prophecy of Joel, fulfilled at Pentecost, declared, "Your sons and daughters shall *prophesy*" (2:17). In the early Church, the functions of prophesying clearly vary (11:28; 21:10; 11; 27:10(see also 1 Corinthians 14:24-25). But the ultimate focus of all prophecy is on Jesus (14:3)—the testimony or the witness of *who* Jesus is and *what* He has done.

Read through the first four chapters of Acts and list the different ways in which the Name of the Lord, or a term or title concerning His person, is expressed. What is the distinct focus of each?

6. The Spirit of Worship

The posture of praise and worship prevails in the life of the young Church. It begins in the upper room, as they spoke "the wonderful works of God" upon their receiving the fullness of the Holy Spirit (2:4, 11). It continues in the daily walk of the congregation (2:46-47).

Perhaps no text in Acts more clearly accentuates the priority and power of worship—that is, "ministering to the Lord"—than what occurred at Antioch as they did so. "As they ministered to the Lord and fasted..." the Holy Spirit disclosed His plan for global evangelism.

It is this text that God used to personally impact my own heart with this understanding: if a worshiping congregation can be developed, the Holy Spirit will move in its midst to achieve soul-winning evangelism at dimensions human promotionalism can never dream of or reach.

7. The Community of Saints

Early in Acts we are introduced to a degree of unselfishness and mutual care that became a confirmation of God's love in the eyes of the watching world (2:44-45; 4:32-37). The disaster of Ananias and Sapphira (5:1-11) is presented as a contradiction of this splendid spirit, and the action of the Holy Spirit in the face of their hypocrisy is powerfully instructive as to the value God places on such care and integrity.

It is instructive to look closely at these texts, and certain lessons accentuate the difference between a *communistic* culture and a *communal* one. The first, the humanistic program of communism, legally requires that all be brought to a common denominator of possessions. But in contrast, the second—the biblical example—invites all to see that none are without need.

That the disciples sold things or brought goods that provided funds for distribution as they were sold (4:36-37) doesn't necessarily mean that each person sold everything he or she had. Rather, they sold things they didn't need in order to care for those who had less.

8. The Message of the Kingdom

There are eight passages in Acts which directly reference "the Kingdom of God" as the undergirding concept of their message. This is consistent with Jesus' preaching (Mark 1:14) and the way He discipled the apostles (Matthew 24:14). The preaching of Jesus as "Messiah" (the Christ) is the proclamation of *The* King; God's King sent to reinstate His rule and divine order in the life and affairs of those who receive Him. What do you surmise from each of the texts in Acts which directly mention "the Kingdom"?

Acts 1:3
Acts 1:6
Acts 8:12
Acts 14:22

Acts 19:8
Acts 20:25
Acts 28:23
Acts 28:31

The Environment of Harvest in
ACTS

9. The Painful Price of Hateful Persecution

The Greek word we translate "witness" or "testimony" is *martureo*, the same word from which we derive the English word "martyr". The history of the Church of Jesus Christ is that it only makes its gain through pain. This is not a legalistic requirement, but it is a historical fact—and there are personal implications for all of us in this regard.

In your reading of and listening to the whole of Acts, begin a list of times people are mocked, criticized, attacked, beaten, stoned, pursued, accused unjustly, ridiculed, rejected, and killed. To note this is not to cultivate a "martyr complex," but it will help you keep perspective on your own times of suffering for the Gospel.

10. The Perplexing Problem of Ethnic Conflict

Two facts shine forth from Acts regarding God's heart for the unity of the peoples of mankind under the rule and reign of His Son, the Messiah Jesus.

First, the outpouring of the Spirit came upon people who instantly caught the attention of men and women from many geographic regions as they heard those who had been Spirit-filled supernaturally praise and worship God in their regional "tongues" (2:4-13). Most Bible scholars agree: this was God's announcement of His will to *reach* all peoples, as well as to *reconcile* all peoples—to Himself first, and to one another as well (see 2 Corinthians 5:16-21; Ephesians 2:11-22).

Second, the strain between the early Jewish and Gentile believers is a struggle point throughout Acts, and reflected in many of the New Testament's epistles. The slowness of many in the Church to respond with a reconciling spirit in those days is a warning to us today—that we let the Holy Spirit work in healing racial and ethnic attitudes, as well as break other yokes of sin that would entrap our lives.

11. The Passionate Pursuit of Dynamic Evangelism

There are a series of maps provided in this small study guide. Go to the passages in Acts where each journey is referenced geographically, and answer these questions:

- What was required in terms of sacrifice or faithfulness to bring the messenger(s) to those he reaches with God's Word?
- What seems to be the motivating force behind the movement to this scene of ministry?
- Of what is the central thrust of the "witness" borne, and how is it delivered?
- What does the Holy Spirit do to confirm the word as it is brought, and what are the results of this evangelistic pursuit?
- What does this episode say to you about your availability to the Holy Spirit's work today?

12. The Preserved Priority of Persistent Prayer

Throughout Acts a theme of prayer prevails. There is hardly a chapter without a recorded prayer meeting or time of prayer!! From the first mention of "one accord" (1:14) to the last use of that term in reference to believers (15:25), the power of that *idea* motivates prayer and generates faith for answers.

"One accord" (Greek, *homothumadon*) means to be at the same degree of concern, to be equally concerned—of one heart and mind. This mindset only settles on souls who move before the Throne of God together in prayer. The massive release of power in the early Church is directly correlated with its unwillingness to be turned aside from its ministry of prayer (e.g., 3:1; 4:24-31; 6:4; 10:9, etc.). Use a concordance to look up each reference to "prayer, praise, worship," etc. in Acts. Note the nature of the situation and see what practical insight you may gain for your own prayer life. (There are at least 35 occurrences of "pray, prayed, prayer," etc. alone.)

Conclusion: The Book of Acts does not reveal a model church, but it does provide cases which model those things that make the Church powerful in every age. The humanness of the saints in that day were as subject to problem and misunderstanding, failure and mistake, as we are today. But they triumphed—mightily. And so may we, as we take their lessons to heart and welcome the same Holy Spirit as our Source of Power—and His Word as our standard of Truth and Wisdom.

Paul's First Missionary
JOURNEY

Nelson's Complete Book of Maps and Charts © 1993, Thomas Nelson, Inc.

PART 2

THE RELEVANT ANSWERS IN ACTS

SCOTT BAUER

Paul's Second Missionary
JOURNEY

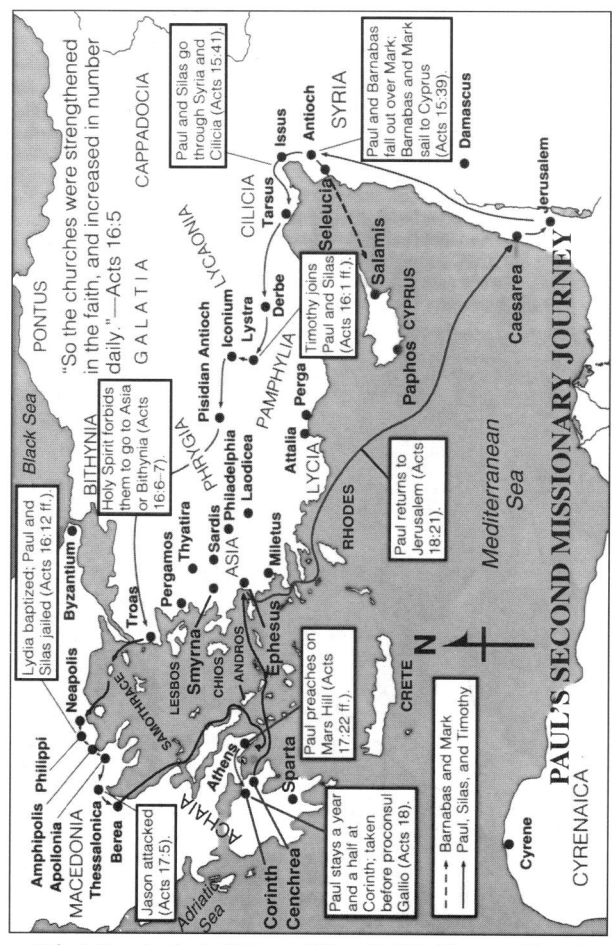

Nelson's Complete Book of Maps and Charts © 1993, Thomas Nelson, Inc.

Answering Questions and
SOLVING PROBLEMS

Jesus and the Power
of the Holy Spirit

The outpouring of the Holy Spirit in the Book of Acts is the single most dramatic event in the post-resurrection life of the disciples, and it is the turning point for the new Church and the history of our world. The frightened followers of Jesus of Nazareth were promised "power when the Holy Spirit has come upon you" (Acts 1:8). And the promise was made by none other than the Lord Jesus Himself. This was by no means a casual comment of encouragement to those who had been faithful; it was the dynamic promise which was to fulfill His purposes from the beginning of time for the salvation of all people.

The Heart
of God's Concern

The Bible is the account of God's love toward His creation. It is a love that cannot be stopped by a resistant sinful world or a hateful adversary. It is based in God's concern and love which are available to us (Acts 15:17). This love is dramatically documented throughout the recorded history of the

Bible, which shows that God has been reaching toward humanity. In the Garden of Eden, God walked and talked with Adam. Since the breaking of this fellowship, God has continually attempted to restore relationship with His sinful creation.

In God's attempt to reach humankind with His love, He has sought out a people to bear witness to His goodness so that the entire world could know His salvation. To Abraham, God declared, "In you all the families of the earth shall be blessed" (Genesis 12:3). The intent of God has never been to focus His interest on only one nation. God's desire has been to rescue those who are willing to trust Him.

God's interest in the nation of Israel was so that it might become a nation of priests to bear witness to the world of His loving intention toward all people (Exodus 19:6). This nation was to be the answer for restoring the worship and knowledge of the true and living God throughout the world. Yet, the failure of Israel to respond to that role is only a part of the continuing story of man's inability to serve God in the power of human flesh and wisdom. Neither the giving of the Law nor the kings and prophets of Israel could effect renewal in Israel itself, much less in the nations of the world.

Apart from the symbolic nature of the construction of the Tabernacle and later the Temple, Israel never accomplished its responsibility to declare the salvation of God to the whole world. In the Temple in Jerusalem was the court of the Gentiles where worshipers could come to present themselves to the Lord. The availability of this access was never communicated to the lost world outside the boundaries of Israel. However, there were hungry souls who acknowledged the God of Israel and were accepted into the worship life of Israel.

But now, with the coming of Pentecost, the task of bringing the salvation of the Lord to the whole world could begin in earnest. Those who had committed their lives to Jesus Christ and had been baptized with the supernatural power of the Holy Spirit were to embark on the ultimate purpose of God in the world—"and you shall be witnesses to Me in Jerusalem, and in all Judea and Samaria, and to the end of the earth" (Acts 1:8).

The desperate needs of humanity could be met only in God's own coming to save His people. The Incarnation of Christ and the atoning work of God on the Cross were God's answer to this eternal problem. But there had to be *something more* for the message of God's love to reach the whole world.

The Power to Reach With God's Love

It is the heart of God's love that brings us to Acts 2 and the outpouring of the Holy Spirit on the disciples. The Lord is about to fulfill His eternal mission in reaching to the world in love. A redeemed people filled with the Holy Spirit will now bear witness to the world of the goodness of God (Acts 1:8).

The baptism with the Holy Spirit directly relates to the ministry of the Lord Jesus: He is the Baptizer. John the Baptist clearly testifies to the unique place of Holy Spirit baptism in the life of the believer. He contrasts his call to repentance and water baptism with the coming of One who will baptize with the Holy Spirit. "John answered saying to all, 'I indeed baptize you with water; but One mightier than I is coming, whose sandal strap I am not worthy to loose. He will baptize you with the Holy Spirit and fire'" (Luke 3:16). This prophetic declaration of John's is predated by Joel's prophecy, eight hundred years before a promise was given to Israel that "I will pour out My Spirit on all flesh."

This remarkable promise has been fulfilled by the outpouring of the Holy Spirit in Acts 2:4. Peter affirms this truth in his Pentecost sermon by quoting the prophet Joel in Acts 2:16-21. This outpouring of the Holy Spirit not only signifies the filling of the Church with power, but it clearly declares that the purpose of this baptism is for the salvation of all people.

The passion of God for the lost brought Jesus into the world, and His sacrifice on the Cross was the means by which we are saved. But it is the outpouring of the Holy Spirit that energizes the Church in its mission to reach to the world with the love of God.

Questions Concerning the Holy Spirit

The critical questions in the Book of Acts relate to the Person and work of the Holy Spirit. The Church has argued in the 20th century over the differences in understanding how God works in His Church. There have been divisions between those who believe that the only work of God in a believer's life takes place at salvation, while others are convinced that a second work of grace occurs with Spirit baptism. These divisions are slowly being erased in the Body of Christ as the growth of the Pentecostal and Charismatic churches continues to bear undeniable fruit both in transformed lives and zeal for evangelism. However, real questions exist as to how God works by the Holy Spirit in the life of a believer.

What is the difference between the Holy Spirit in salvation and Holy Spirit baptism?

The Bible defines the redeemed as those in whom "the Spirit of God dwells" (Romans 8:9). The Presence of the Holy Spirit is what brings God's grace to work in the life of a believer. Therefore, every person who has received Christ as his or her Savior has also become indwelt by the Holy Spirit (Colossians 1:27; Revelation 3:20). This is the most obvious rendering of John 20:22. Jesus encounters the disciples immediately following the resurrection and, after assuring them of His physical resurrection, He confers a most important blessing—He breathes on them, and says to them, "Receive the Holy Spirit."

Some claim that Jesus' words merely anticipated the work of Pentecost in Acts 2. Others insist that John is simply rendering a different and less dramatic account of Acts 2. This seems totally beyond reason. First, John is not confused about the timing of the event. Pentecost happened fifty days after the resurrection. John clearly states that this event happened "the same day (of the resurrection) at evening" (John 20:19). Second, if Jesus had meant for them to receive the Spirit only symbolically, His words would have indicated that. However, He immediately granted privileges to His disciples based on the experience of having received the Holy Spirit.

This encounter in John 20 is the Presence of the Holy Spirit in the new birth of the disciples (Titus 3:5). It is not to be confused with the coming of Holy Spirit power and fullness in Acts 2:4. Following this encounter with the disciples, Jesus instructs them to "tarry in the city of Jerusalem until you are endued with power from on high" (Luke 24:49). This power encounter with the Holy Spirit is described later as the baptism with the Holy Spirit (Acts 1:5; 11:16) and fulfills the prophecy of John the Baptist in Luke 3:16.

Holy Spirit baptism is a separate work of the Holy Spirit "filling" (2:4) a person for the purpose of supernatural power for witness and ministry (1:8). This is completely apart from the work of salvation. Acts 2:38 suggests the pattern for believers: "Repent, and let every one of you be baptized in the name of Jesus Christ…and you shall receive the gift of the Holy Spirit." Repentance, faith, and baptism are all united in the understanding of the Early Church as the thorough witness of a person's faith in Christ. The personal decision followed by a public commitment of water baptism was the way for all believers to indicate their faith. The gift of the Holy Spirit concerns His presence and power in a new life. However, there is more.

Acts 8:15 illustrates the point of those who had come to genuine faith in the midst of the Samarian revival and had been water baptized in the Name of

Jesus Christ (8:12-13). However, Peter and John came to the revival asking the question concerning their having "received the Holy Spirit." Though believers in Christ and committed through water baptism, they were still missing the supernatural fullness of the Holy Spirit, which they then received at the hands of the Apostles.

Holy Spirit baptism is a separate work apart from salvation which empowers a person for supernatural service to the Lord. There is one important consideration that follows on this truth. Spirit baptism is not a reflection of superior spirituality or improved character. It is a gift from God received by faith for those willing to open to it. There are many scars in the Body of Christ over the subject of those who have received this Spirit baptism, presuming to be superior to those who have yet to experience it. The Lord does not rate our relationship with Him based on our experience, but upon our love and faithfulness. As we encourage people to open to the power of the Holy Spirit, our humble invitation is to all those who hunger for more of what God has to offer them.

Doesn't the Bible say there is only one baptism in Ephesians 4:5?

"There is one body and one Spirit…one hope …one Lord, one faith, one baptism; one God and Father of all" (Eph. 4:4-6). The baptism referred to in this context is water baptism. The point of the passage is that there is only one Church, one Body of Christ, and there is only one way to publicly enter it—through water baptism. Paul writes in 1 Corinthians 12:13, "For by one Spirit we were all baptized into one body—whether Jews or Greeks." Notice in this baptism the "baptizer" is the Holy Spirit. In Holy Spirit baptism, the Baptizer is the Lord Jesus Himself (Luke 3:16; John 16:7). There is never any sense in which this passage alters the other things spoken concerning Holy Spirit baptism.

Isn't speaking in tongues simply speaking "other languages"? (Acts 2:8-11)

Two things are very clear from this passage. First, the tongues of Pentecost were a supernatural work of God in the lives of those in the Upper Room. They were unlearned languages which the disciples spoke and which God used to witness to those gathered in Jerusalem on that day. The second thing that took place is that the tongues on this day were proclaiming praise to God: "We hear them speaking in our own tongues the wonderful works of God" (Acts 2:11). Many want to suggest that the only use of tongues is for supernatural proclamation for the purpose of witness. However, this is not in keeping with the entire record of the Book of Acts.

In Acts 10:46, the Gentiles who were gathered in the house of Cornelius were listening to Peter preach when "they heard them speak with tongues and magnify God." There was no one in the room who needed the witness of Jesus Christ for salvation. Peter and those with him were already believers. Apparently, these tongues were not only unknown to the speaker, but to the listener as well. First Corinthians 14:2-4 further advances our understanding of the purpose of tongues. It is a language known only to God for it is directed toward Him, and it benefits the speaker with personal edification in his or her personal life and walk with God.

What about Ananias and Sapphira in Acts 5?

The question resolves to one simple matter—does God kill people? It is clear that the Bible teaches it is the way of the devil "to steal, and to kill, and to destroy" (John 10:10). Jesus contrasts His own mission in the same verse: "I have come that they may have life, and that they may have it more abundantly." It is neither the nature nor the way of Jesus to kill people.

There are, however, incidents in Scripture when people have pridefully resisted God and His work and have suffered for it. Having heard the account of David's anger toward Nabal because of Nabal's hard-hearted arrogance, it says "his heart died within him." Scripture is very clear that, "through the Lord's mercies we are not consumed" (Lamentations 3:22). Malachi 3 asserts that the changeless God is the reason that the children of faith are not consumed. God has never changed His mode of operation. Yet, when people live outside the boundaries of His ability to bless and keep them, they make themselves vulnerable to the weakness of their flesh and the prowling, consuming work of the adversary.

How does God direct your life? (Acts 16:6)

Paul and Silas were set to preach the Gospel in Asia, and "they were forbidden by the Holy Spirit"

(Acts 16:6). This opens the way to a broad subject of how people receive direction from God. There are three basic ways: First, the Bible often gives specific direction about matters over which there is no question—the Ten Commandments in Exodus 20 represent this kind of direction; second, God leads us through a way of faith and trust—"without faith it is impossible to please God" (Hebrews 11:6); third, God gives us specific direction by the Holy Spirit. We are told in this passage (Acts 16:6) how the Lord forbade them to go to Asia—whether through circumstance, improved opportunity elsewhere, or a supernatural intervention in the understanding of Paul and Silas. However, one thing is apparent from the text: it was obvious God was leading them away from ministry in Asia.

Many people struggle over direction in their lives. God's people are called to live by faith, as those who pray and seek God's heart and direction. We are also people of good sense and reason. God expects us to exercise both our faith and common sense to the fullest capacity. And, when He wants us to change what we are doing, He will break into the affairs of our lives in a dramatic way so that we will know for certain His direction for us. Acts 16:6 should be a comfort for all those who want to be about the business of God with confidence. Paul and Silas were heading off for ministry—certainly there is nothing wrong with that! But God redirected their focus to something that would become more profitable and in keeping with His purpose for them.

This should be a matter of great confidence to every believer. God is interested in the affairs of His children. We can know that as we seek to serve Him, He will direct us to the place of maximum fruitfulness as we acknowledge His way and welcome His guidance.

Jesus at Work in
ACTS

Jesus' direct intervention in the Book of Acts can be separated into two categories: First, He intervenes directly in lives so that they can be turned around and second, He offers specific direction and encouragement for the mission immediately ahead. There are four specific incidents that we will look at that record Jesus' encounters with people in the Book of Acts.

Jesus' Instructions Concerning the Holy Spirit (Acts 1:4-8)

This famous passage informs us that the baptism with the Holy Spirit is directly related to the empowering of the Church for ministry and witness. The crucial issues relate to the availability of this power for everyone ("they were all filled," 2:4) and the instruction that the witness of the Church could now be advanced to the whole world. It is critical for every believer to understand his or her own place of responsibility to both receive this "power when the Holy Spirit has come upon you," and to receive the call to bold witness and service to the world. God is not calling us to serve beyond the measure to which He will personally empower us. But He does expect us to advance the Kingdom to the full extent of our influence in our world.

Jesus meets Saul; Jesus directs a man (Acts 9:2-16,22; 26:14-18)

Jesus' confrontation with Saul on the road to Damascus is as dramatic a revelation of the Lord as is found in Scripture. Saul's response to the miracle appearance of Jesus to him opens the way to his becoming the Apostle to the Gentiles. However, Saul did not begin that way.

Saul's opposition to Jesus in Acts is characterized by the murder of Stephen. The first martyr of the Church is directly related to Saul's hatred for Christians and their persecution at his hand. It is the loving intervention of Jesus Himself that turned Saul's life around. At the same time, Jesus appears to Ananias, a godly leader in the Church at Damascus. Without this miracle intervention, Ananias would not have received Saul as a brother in the Lord and assisted him in beginning his life in Christ. In this way, the most significant convert of the Church in the first century comes to faith in the Lord, and his life will bless the world.

Peter's vision from the Lord; Jesus opens the door to His Church (Acts 10:13-15)

This is a crucial moment in the life of the Church. This encounter with Peter opens the way for Gentiles to be added to the Church. The mission of the Church is clarified and expanded beyond the limits that were conceivable to Peter at that time.

Nothing less than this personal, supernatural moment would have convinced Peter of the necessity to minister to the Gentiles. Now the Church is opened to *all people*.

Paul at Corinth; Jesus promises revival in the city (Acts 18:9-10)

After Paul was rebuffed in Corinth by the Jews in the synagogue, he moved next door and began to preach at the house of Justus. Many responded to the message of salvation; however, Jesus' message of comfort to Paul also included a strong exhortation: "I have many people in this city." Paul's stay in Corinth was 18 months long. This is an extended time, considering Paul stayed in most places for only a very short time.

Paul's direction to Rome; Jesus extends His Kingdom (Acts 23:11)

After being challenged and put on trial by Jewish rulers in Jerusalem, Paul was visited in the night by Jesus and told he would go to bear witness of Christ in Rome. This encounter is particularly significant in that the Jews had decided to ambush Paul while he was to be transported by the Romans to Caesarea. The unveiling of the plans of the Jewish leaders (23:16) spared Paul's life. The Lord protects His people so that they may accomplish their ministry of service. This opened the way for the Gospel to come to the heart of the power center of the world.

Holy Spirit Power in
ACTS

No book in the Bible has more drama or supernatural power. The Book of Acts gives us the history of the first century Church, but it also shows us that the Church was conceived by the Holy Spirit's work of rebirth in each person and His power to convince the world of Jesus Christ. Throughout this book there is an awesome display of power; all of it directed for one purpose—to advance the Church and equip and empower God's people for ministry.

We have already examined the "Pentecost power surge" when three thousand were added to the Church. However, following Pentecost there is a continual miracle presence of the Holy Spirit that was not only meant for the first century, but is available for the Church today.

Miracle Healings (Acts 3:7; 5:15; 8:7; 9:34; 9:40; 16:18; 19:11-12; 20:9-10; 28:8-9)

Throughout the Book of Acts, miracle healings and deliverances are abundant. They were neither aberrations to the normal flow of the life of the Church nor were they solely for the purpose of establishing the Church. Healings happened in the early Church because there were sick people, and the compassion that was witnessed in Jesus' ministry continued through the ministry of His Body, the Church.

The miracle presence of the Holy Spirit in the Church is not simply expressed in the ministry of a few apostles. The extension of ministry in Acts 6 to those who were called to serve illustrates the empowering of those "full of the Holy Spirit" (6:3). This same power is available in the Church today. Miracles, signs, and wonders proliferate as people continue to pray with power and minister in faith.

Earthquakes and Prison Breaks (Acts 4:31; 12:7; 16:26)

Whenever the Apostles were imprisoned or intimidated, the Lord had a plan to both encourage and release them. In fact, earthquakes are recorded in Acts 4:31 and 16:26. Both were supernatural signs to the Church of God's presence, power, and purpose being sustained in the mission of the Church. The only exception to this is when prison suited the purpose of God to propel Paul into the final ministry assignment of his life in Rome.

There are also recorded two supernatural prison breaks in Acts: one mentioned above in Acts 16, the other the result of an angelic intervention for Peter in Acts 12. Clearly, the Book of Acts is loaded with enough drama and a crystal clear message—*nothing can stop the ministry of God's Church!*

The Gifts of the Holy Spirit at Work

From the very beginning of the Church's ministry to the world, there has been an impressive array of supernatural ministry gifts to accomplish the task of the Church. **Tongues** were not merely a miracle sign of Pentecost, but they were also used for the purpose of a God-anointed witness to the lost. **Prophecy** is continually given throughout the book, both in the sense of anointed proclamation (Acts

4:33) and in terms of declaring the future intentions of God (Acts 21:11); thereby offering confirmation to what was already present in the hearts of those who led the Church. **Healings**, as mentioned above, happened in abundance. Words of **Knowledge** (9:11) and **Wisdom** (6:10; 22:18,21) display the tireless effort of God to keep His people on track for His purpose. **Miracles** also witnessed to the incredible power of the Holy Spirit in the Church. The demonstration of this kind of extraordinary working of God in the Church is the way for the people of God to live. Often we carelessly use the word "miracle" to describe any unusual kindness of God. Miracles are truly acts of God beyond the realm of human ability and comprehension in order to bring His life into the circumstance (9:40; 20:9-10). **Discerning of spirits** (Acts 16:16) is a gift at work in the Church not simply for "knowledge" in a situation. It is for the deliverance of people from the destructive power of demons at work in their lives. Without this deliverance, people would suffer at the hands of devilish power and never come into the blessing of God. **Faith** was present in conjunction with a word of knowledge concerning Paul and Barnabas' ministry assignment to the Gentiles (Acts 13:2). This missionary endeavor is the first of its kind as the Church intentionally reaches out to people, nations, and cultures radically different from their own. That same gift of faith is necessary in the Church today to continually press the outer boundaries of our own comfort zones to reach others with God's love.

The Church was born in Holy Spirit power, and

its mission can be accomplished only with the same. It is a temptation to read the Book of Acts as either a history of another time, with no relation to our lives today, or as a presumption that God's marvelous power is only received by His truly special servants. Both are perversions of truth. The adversary of our souls would like nothing better than to see the Church bereft of Holy Spirit resource simply because the theology of men declares that God's power is for another era. It is an equally devastating lie that persuades people not to live in all the resources the Holy Spirit would provide for them if they would simply ask for and serve with the power that has been promised them.

The world that we live in is desperate for God's power. Human agencies, governments, and programs offer no solution to the longing in the hearts of every person. Material wealth is an empty substitute for the presence of Jesus Christ. So, the Lord has outfitted His Church with every tool and every spiritual weapon necessary to break the strongholds of darkness and to minister the life of Jesus Christ to our immediate circle of concern and responsibility. Let's rejoice and live in that power! Amen!

Paul's Third Missionary
JOURNEY

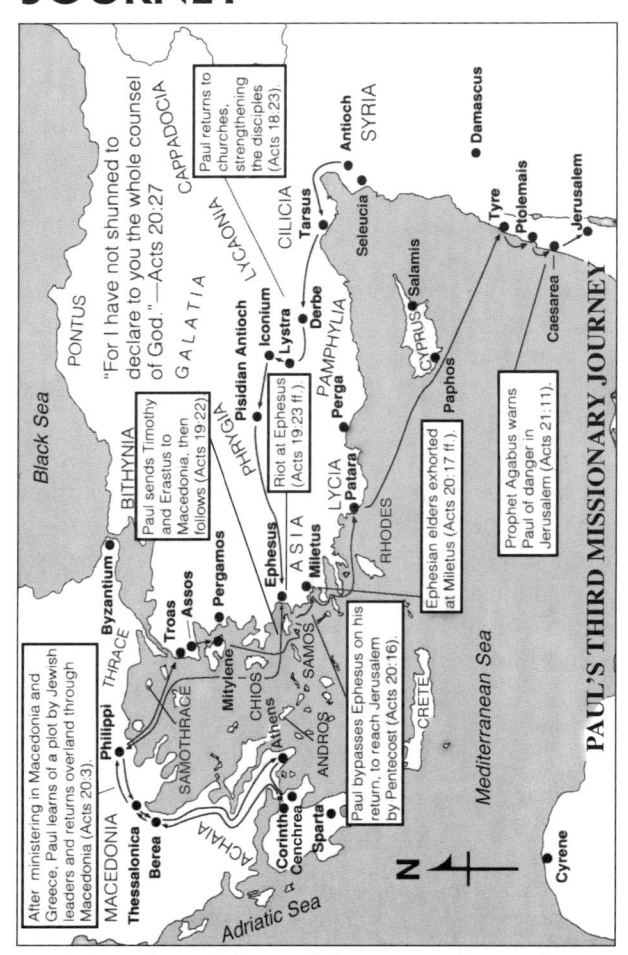

Nelson's Complete Book of Maps and Charts © 1993, Thomas Nelson, Inc.

PART 3

PRACTICAL WISDOM FROM ACTS

JACK HAMILTON

Paul's Fourth Missionary
JOURNEY

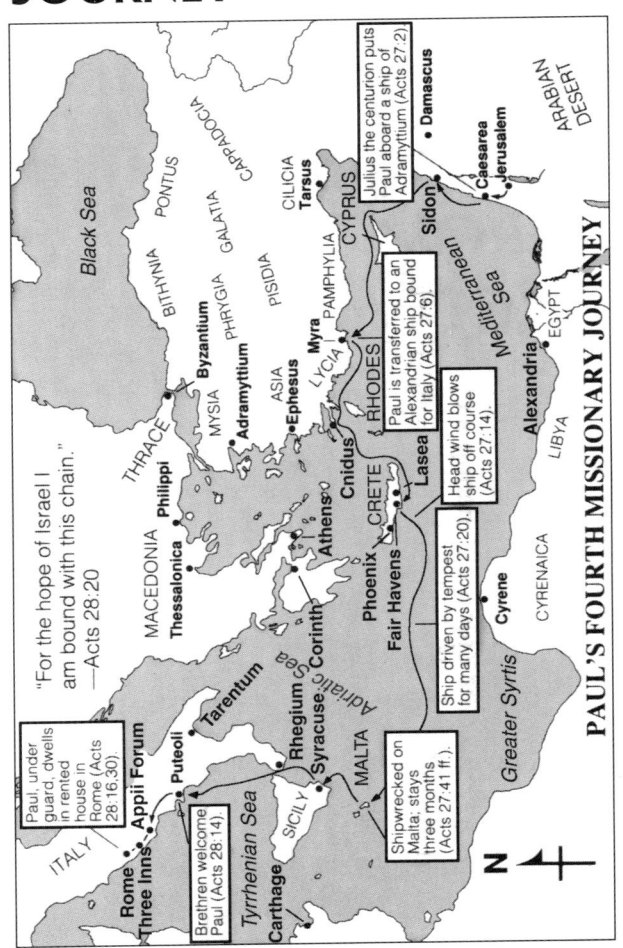

Nelson's Complete Book of Maps and Charts © 1993, Thomas Nelson, Inc.

Relational Living in the
COVENANTS

The title of this book of the Bible is a verb. Designated as *Praxeis*, it is the summary of the first three decades of how people, in cooperation with the Holy Spirit, managed the unthinkable. It contains the accounts of how a small band of men and women faithfully bore testimony to the work of Jesus Christ and the effect it is having on the world to this very day. These heroic exploits were the continuation of the ministry of Jesus through those whom He entrusted with widening the message of the Gospel of the Kingdom and its power to the world of all humanity.

While the record contains the history of the early expansion of the Gospel, it also gives insight on adopting similar motives, as well as methods, for living out the witness of Christ in this contemporary time. The power of the biographical information is that it gives a view of the <u>ethos</u> that compelled the men and women of the Book of Acts, along with a description of their <u>exploits</u>. It is the insight gained from understanding the moral nature and guiding beliefs of the Early Church that, when embraced by believers today, will result in the same impact on the culture and nations of this era as then.

Imagine being on the Mount of Olives, just outside Jerusalem and across the Kidron Valley. It is the end of forty days following the resurrection of Jesus. There have been occasional encounters between the Risen Lord and His band of followers during this interval. Jesus has once and for all settled their concerns about His being the Messiah (Christ). Convinced that their allegiance has been properly placed, they are eager to begin the quest of the ages. They are anticipating the inception of His Messianic reign and ask Him, "Lord, will You at this time restore the kingdom to Israel?" (Acts 1:6).

They are not quite ready for His reply. "It is not for you to know times or seasons which the Father has put in His own authority" (1:7). He then gives them a **promise** and a **purpose**. "But you shall receive power when the Holy Spirit has come upon you; and you shall be witnesses to Me in Jerusalem, and in all Judea and Samaria, and to the end of the earth" (1:8). Jesus is then physically taken up into heaven. Amazed at both His words and ascension, they stand in awe viewing this wonder. It takes the appearance of two angels, who underscore that He will come again in like manner as He ascended (physically), to get them to move from the mountain to get ready for an incredible personal transformation (1:10-11). And upon returning to Jerusalem, to an upper room, they continue to gather together in one accord for prayer and supplications, waiting for what was promised (1:4-5,12-14).

The Promise in
ACTS

*"But you shall receive **power** when the Holy Spirit has come upon you…"*

The Holy Spirit is not a force—some impersonal entity that someone may employ as one would utilize nuclear energy. The Holy Spirit is a person with whom another person can have a relationship. He has the capacities of personality, such as reason, emotion, and will and on this basis interacts with people. It is an expanded relationship with the Holy Spirit that Jesus promises His followers.

The prototype of the Spirit's activities is well established in Jesus Himself. Jesus' life as a human was the work of the life-giving Spirit (Matthew 1:20; Luke 1:35). And it is not until His unique anointing at the Jordan River, when the Spirit comes upon Him, that Jesus begins to do the miraculous things that astound people over the course of the next three years of His life (Matthew 3:16; Mark 1:10; Luke 3:22; John 1:32-33).

In similar fashion, the life given to people who believe and receive Christ is generated by the Holy Spirit (John 3:5,6). This gift of life from the Spirit now enables the believer to overcome the consequences of sin and death (Romans 8:2-3). The believer is now charged with a ministry mandate which includes both a declaration and a demonstration of the continuation of Christ's work of salvation in the world today (Mark 16:15-20).

The command of Jesus is to wait for the Promise (Luke 24:49). It is the fundamental fact that the work of God's Kingdom is not a matter of human energy. The zeal, ability, or training of an individual will not accomplish what is inherent in the commission to take Christ's testimony and ministry to all humanity. As people are to live by the Spirit to manifest the life of Jesus (Romans 8:14), they are to minister to others in the same manner of power as Christ (John 14:12).

The declaration of John the Baptist that Jesus is the Baptizer with the Holy Spirit and fire (Luke 3:16) is a preparatory statement for the release of the Promise. If people are to minister like Christ, they will have to experience a Spirit anointing, too (Luke 4:18-19). And it is Jesus who will key the release of the Holy Spirit upon His followers. Promised by the Father and administered by the Son, the Baptism in the Spirit is essential and Jesus prepares believers for this divine eventuality.

When the Spirit is given in this fashion, a new power is available to the recipient—the power to do. Healing the sick, casting out demons, speaking in tongues unlearned, ministering with signs and wonders—all of these and more are what disciples are energized to accomplish when the Spirit comes upon them. As Jesus was anointed with the Spirit and power, so His followers, in any age, will be similarly anointed and enabled to carry on His ministry.

The Purpose in
ACTS

*"...you shall be **witnesses** to Me in Jerusalem, and in all Judea and Samaria, and to the end of the earth."*

The promise of power is to accomplish the purpose. The purpose is to become Christ's witness. And the witness is to operate in an increasing sphere of influence. As with the early disciples, so it is with those of this era. The testimony of Jesus and the release of His ministry to humanity are the sole responsibility of followers of Christ. This is the reason His Church is in the world, to fulfill the commission that will only conclude at the *Parousia*, His Second Coming.

There are at least three things to note about being a witness of Christ. First, a witness is someone who acknowledges that the testimony is true to experience. In a court of law, the account given cannot be hearsay, but the evidence must be in accordance with what has actually happened to the one testifying. One of the most potent examples of this is found in John 9, where the healed blind man, when pressed about Jesus, states, "One thing I know: that though I was blind now I see. If this Man were not from God, He could do nothing" (John 9:25, 33). A witness does not say things like, "I think so," or "It could be," but with firm conviction, "I know!" The person with the experience is never at the mercy of the person with the argument.

Second, the real witness is not one of just words but of deeds. Living out words is the most validating action of beliefs. "Show me your faith without your works, and I will show you my faith by my works" (James 2:18b). The Lord Jesus comforts all disciples of any era when He is "…working with them and confirming the word through the accompanying signs" (Mark 16:20). William Barclay, in *The Daily Bible Study Series on Acts*, recites that when Stanley had discovered Livingstone in Central Africa and had spent some time with him, he said, "If I had been with him any longer I would have been compelled to be a Christian and he never spoke to me about it at all." When words and deeds are congruent, the witness of a life is irresistible.

Third, in the language of the New Testament Greek, the word for witness and martyr is the same *(martus)*. Jesus certainly implies this when He said, "If anyone desires to come after Me, let him deny himself and take up his cross, and follow Me. For whoever desires to save his life will lose it, and whoever loses his life for My sake will find it" (Matthew 16:24-25). A witness must be ready for any eventuality and be loyal no matter what the cost.

As when this purpose was initially declared, so it is in today's world. People are desperate. Their lives are filled with every consequence of sin's ravaging effect. It is the witness of contemporary believers that will affect this condition as they declare and demonstrate the salvation that the Lord Jesus Christ offers humanity everywhere. This is the purpose proposed by Christ.

EXAMPLES OF POWER LIVING

In the Book of Acts there are examples of behavior and belief by the principal personalities. The spotlight on their witness affords a model for believers of this hour. As they faced circumstances confronting everyone at one time or another, their actions and words are helpful as the Church continues to live in the dynamic of the Holy Spirit. The character portrayals of Peter, Paul, Stephen, Philip, Cornelius, and Barnabas will illustrate how the empowerment of ordinary people enabled them to accomplish an extraordinary task.

POWER OVER CONFUSION

Confusion is a common human experience. Just when people think they have figured something out, another something is thrown into the mix that creates a bewildering element. Peter's life seems to be challenged with making sense out of some confusing events. As one of the first group to be baptized with the Holy Spirit, it falls to him to explain what is going on. From this time on, the Book of Acts tells of how Peter was a man empowered to explain to others the works of God among them that tended to be perplexing.

A. Confusion Over a Fulfilled Promise
"'Whatever could this mean?'" (2:12).

B. Confusion Over a Wondrous Miracle
"…they were filled with wonder and amazement …greatly amazed…greatly disturbed…" (3:10-11; 4:2).

C. **Confusion Over an Offering**
    "So great fear came upon all the church and upon all who heard these things" (5:11).
D. **Confusion Over a Vision**
    "…Peter wondered within himself what this vision which he had seen meant…" (10:17).
E. **Confusion Over a Jailbreak**
    "But they said to her, 'You are beside yourself!' …when they opened the door and saw him, they were astonished" (12:15-16).

POWER OVER LIES

False accusations are extremely difficult to defend. This is especially true when a conspiracy is in place. When a threat to the status quo arose, a group of religious leaders plotted against Stephen. The motive behind their apprehension of Stephen was based in his being a threat to their positions. Having induced some people to lie about what they had heard, these leaders of the Synagogue of the Freedmen stirred up the people, the elders, and the scribes to seize him and bring false allegations against him (6:9, 11-12). Stephen, with the wisdom of the Spirit, unmasks their lies with a heroic defense and death.

A. **Lies Deny Faith**
    "'The God of glory appeared to our father Abraham…Get out of your country…come to a land that I will show you…'Then He gave him the covenant of circumcision…" (7:2,3,8).
B. **Lies Frustrate Grace**
    "And the patriarchs, becoming envious, sold

Joseph into Egypt. But God was with him" (7:9).
C. Lies Lead to Rebellion
"This is that Moses…the one who received the living oracles to give to us, whom our fathers would not obey, but rejected" (7:37-39).
D. Lies Produce Stubbornness
"You stiff-necked and uncircumcised in heart and ears! You always resist the Holy Spirit; as your fathers did, so do you" (7:51).
E. Lies Are Overcome by the Spirit of Forgiveness
"But he, being full of the Holy Spirit…cried out with a loud voice, 'Lord, do not charge them with this sin'" (7:55, 60).

POWER OVER PREJUDICE

Prejudice and bias distort truth. How others are viewed and thought about will make a difference as to how the witness of Christ will be distributed. If one sees the Church as exclusive, then the point of the Cross of Christ is grossly misunderstood. It usually takes some extraordinary event to push people beyond their bigotry. The Early Church had paid little notice to the commission to take the witness to everyone. Not until a reign of persecution arose against them did they scatter, going everywhere preaching the Word (8:4). It was Philip and Peter who spearheaded this new thrust of outreach which would help to secure the inclusive nature of Christ's salvation. The principal manifestation that gave this new effort God's approval was an outpouring of the Holy Spirit. Whether in Samaria, Gaza, or a Roman household in Caesarea, the Spirit of God was expanding the sphere of influence which the Gospel was to have. And prejudice was what was being challenged.

A. Prejudice Defeated Through Revival
"Then Philip went down to the city of Samaria and preached Christ to them. And multitudes with one accord heeded the things spoken by Philip, hearing and seeing the miracles which he did. For unclean spirits, crying with a loud voice, came out of many who were possessed; and many who were paralyzed and lame were healed. Now when the apostles…heard that Samaria had received the word of God, they sent Peter and John to them…that they might receive the Holy Spirit" (8:5-7,14-15).

B. Prejudice Overcome Through Obedience
"Now an angel of the Lord spoke to Philip, saying, 'Arise and go toward the south…' This is desert…Then the Spirit said to Philip, 'Go near and overtake this chariot'… Now when they came up out of the water, the Spirit of the Lord caught Philip away'"… (8:26, 29, 39).

C. Prejudice Destroyed by Revelation
"Cornelius…a devout man and one who feared God…saw clearly in a vision an angel of God coming in and saying…'Your prayers and your alms have come up for a memorial before God.' The next day…Peter went up on the housetop to pray…he fell into a trance and saw heaven opened and an object like a great sheet …descending to him and let down to the earth. While Peter was still speaking…the Holy Spirit

fell upon all those who heard the word" (10:1-4, 9-11, 44).

POWER OVER RESISTANCE

Folklore speaks of the clash of the irresistible force and the immovable object. Such is not the case when the Holy Spirit exerts His power in any given situation. Saul of Tarsus encountered the Holy Spirit at the martyrdom of Stephen. While he resisted for a season, his resolve was destroyed on the road to Damascus (Chapter 9). The Church has grave reservations about the authenticity of this man's conversion. Barnabas recognized the Spirit's work in Saul's life and became his benefactor, and later on, his partner (9:27, 13:2). The endorsement of Barnabas, a Spirit-filled and Spirit-led man, eroded the resistance of the Church toward this apostle in the making.

Later Saul, who becomes Paul, is sent out by the Holy Spirit as a missionary. He encounters resistance to the witness of Christ every place he goes. Paul is not stopped or discouraged, for he is filled with the Holy Spirit (9:17; 13:9) and in almost every region, throughout his lifetime, churches are established no matter what the resistance. Individuals come to Christ through his witness, many being healed or delivered from demon activity as well. Political, social, cultural, or spiritual resistance is no match for the power of the Spirit in the life of this apostle who once led active resistance against the One to whom he is now yielded, for he is sure that he belongs to God and is serving Him (27:23).

A. **Overcoming Individual Resistance**
"Then Saul, still breathing threats and murder against the disciples of the Lord…fell to the ground…said, 'Who are You, Lord?' And the Lord said, 'I am Jesus…'" (9:1, 4-5).

B. **Overcoming Spiritual Resistance**
"…a certain slave girl possessed with a spirit of divination…followed Paul…Paul, greatly annoyed, turned and said to the spirit, 'I command you in the name of Jesus Christ to come out of her.' And he came out that very hour" (16:16-18).

C. **Overcoming Philosophical Resistance**
"Now while Paul waited…at Athens…certain Epicurean and Stoic philosophers encountered him. Some men joined him and believed…" (17:16, 18, 34).

D. **Overcoming Community Resistance**
"Paul…came to Ephesus. Now God worked unusual miracles by the hands of Paul…about that time there arose a great commotion about the Way. After the uproar had ceased, Paul called the disciples to him…"(19:1; 11:23; 20:1).

E. **Overcoming Religious Resistance**
"…the Jews from Asia, seeing him in the temple, stirred up the whole crowd… 'Men and brethren, I have lived in all good conscience before God'…And the high priest Anaias commanded those who stood by him to strike him on the mouth" (21:27; 23:1-2).

F. **Overcoming Cultural Resistance**
"Now when we came to Rome…many came to him at his lodging, to whom he explained and

solemnly testified of the kingdom of God…And some were persuaded" (28:16, 23, 24).

WITNESS AND POWER

The beginning of the Book of Acts tells of the ascending Lord, the descending Holy Spirit, and the expanding Church. Sent as witnesses and endued with power, the followers of Christ made a deep penetration into a world held captive by sin and alienation from God. Their work is not finished, for this generation of believers must complete the task. The same Lord Jesus compels today's Church to speak boldly and live faithfully. The same Holy Spirit empowers believers to do mighty works as confirmation of the truth and liberation of the needy.

The Acts of the Apostles presents a narrative about models for dynamic living. The Church of today must continue to consistently represent what so clearly is demonstrated by this first wave of heroes.

Additional Ministry Resources

Explore God's Word with Dr. Jack Hayford!

THE LIVING WAY
BIBLE STUDY SERIES:
THE BOOK OF ACTS

Dr. Hayford teaches verse by verse and precept upon precept in this dynamic expositional series. The twelve audio tapes come in an attractive vinyl album with study notes.

SC355

*Retrace Pastor Jack Hayford's
own spiritual journey!*

THE BEAUTY OF SPIRITUAL LANGUAGE

In this devotional, Pastor Jack helps readers see both the maturity of a contemporary Christian leader and the experience God intends for all His children. This book will debunk common myths, remove the fears, and dissolve the stereotypes surrounding the Biblical practice of speaking in tongues. *Softcover* **BSL02**

Plunge through ancient seas with the physician Luke (Dean Jones) as he tells about the danger, struggle, and triumph that mark the birth of the Christian church.

ACTS VIDEO SERIES
Word for Word from the N.I.V. Text

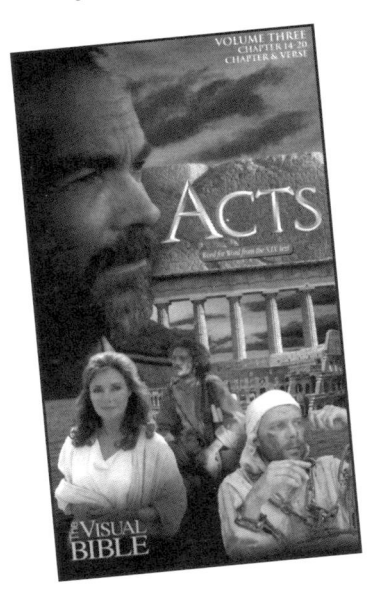

As Luke's powerful narrative brings the Acts of the Holy Spirit through the Apostles to life, you will gain new insight into the compassionate love that unites the fellowship of believers. **VBACT**

Features Dean Jones, James Brolin, Jennifer O'Neill, and Bruce Marchiano

Want the Best Study Bible on the Market Today?

The
SPIRIT-FILLED LIFE BIBLE
may be what you're looking for!

The Spirit-Filled Life Bible is a powerful resource for enriching your relationship with Jesus Christ. Faith-filled, prophetic, and Spirit-empowered insights are featured in this one-of-a-kind study Bible. Here, in the light of God's Word, you will discover a Spirit-filled life rich in Godly characteristics.

This 2200-page, magnificently bound Bible is available from Living Way Ministries in either Burgundy or black genuine leather, and a classic hardback library edition—which is also available in English or Spanish.

Hardback Library Edition: **SFLHB**
Burgundy Genuine Leather: **SFLBG**
Black Genuine Leather: **SGLBK**

A one-of-a-kind resource!

Understand the Power in Baptism.

BAPTISM: FREEDOM AND FULLNESS IN CHRIST

In these two audio tapes, Pastor Jack stresses the importance and practice of baptism in water and baptism with the Holy Spirit. **SC508**

This two-tape mini album is small enough for pocket or purse!

Unveil the Keys to Scripture!

HAYFORD'S BIBLE HANDBOOK

Hayford's Bible Handbook is an unparalleled resource that uniquely unveils the keys to Scripture, providing not only a wealth of information, but also a spiritual stimulus that will encourage your faith and service to Christ.

It unlocks Scripture with:
- Illuminating surveys of each book of the Bible.
- Helpful illustrations, time lines, maps, and charts.
- A complete Visual Survey of the Bible.
- An Encyclopedia Dictionary with over 1,300 entries that address subjects of particular interest to Spirit-filled believers.

This guide opens the riches of Scripture with a unique focus on practical ministry in the Holy Spirit's power—all to deepen your life in Christ. **HBH**

This guide will open the riches of Scripture and deepen your life in Christ!

*Down-to-Earth Insight
for students of all ages!*

SPIRIT-FILLED LIFE BIBLE FOR STUDENTS

The Spirit-Filled Life Bible for students is a new dynamic tool that can help students deepen their spiritual roots and grow in Christ. This New King James Version resource for students offers real-life, down-to-earth insight for living the Christian life in today's world. General Editor Jack Hayford and nearly a dozen contributing authors have provided:

- Hundreds of helpful annotations.
- Maps and charts.
- Articles on major Bible themes.

This is a practical gift for students of any age who want to learn and live God's Word by the Power of His Spirit.

Softcover **SFLBS**

*This practical gift will help
your favorite student learn and live God's Word
by the Holy Spirit's power!*

ORDER FORM

Qty.	Item	Code	Price	Total

Postage and Handling

$0.00 - $9.99 .... $2.95
$10.00 - $29.99 .... $4.95
$30.00 - $59.99 .... $6.95
$60.00 and up ...... Free *(In the U.S.)*
All orders outside the USA .... $8, plus 20% of Subtotal

Subtotal _____
Add 8.25% sales tax to CA orders _____
Shipping and Handling _____
Donation (Optional) _____
Total _____

Name _____

Street Address _____

City _____ State _____ Zip _____

Phone Number (_____) _____

Method of Payment: ❑ Check or Money Order ❑ Visa ❑ MC

_____ / _____-_____-_____ / _____
Signature   Card Number   Exp. Date

MINISTRY RESOURCES
LIVING · WAY MINISTRIES

14820 Sherman Way, Van Nuys, CA 91405-2233

Please call for prices and ordering information:
1-800-776-8180 • 1-818-779-8480
www.livingway.org

Please include your remittance (U.S. currency only) with order.
Make check or money order payable to Living Way Ministries.